INSPIRE YOUR BUYERS

GO TO MARKET WITH A STORY THAT SIZZLES

BRUCE SCHEER

Inspire Your Buyers: Go to Market with A Story That Sizzles
Published by InspireYourBuyers.com
Seattle, Washington

ISBN: 979-8-9872148-0-0
BUSINESS & ECONOMICS / Sales & Selling / General

Cover and Interior design by Victoria Wolf, wolfdesignandmarketing.com. Copyright owned by Bruce Scheer.

Printed in the United States of America.

Inspire Your Buyers

CONTENTS

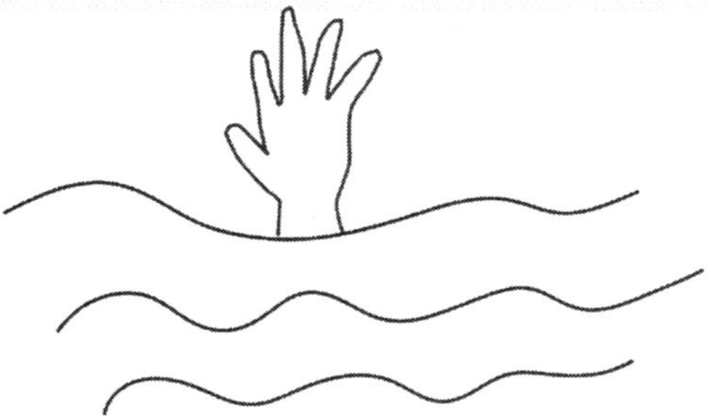

INTRODUCTION

IN THE LEAD-UP TO THE 2020 PANDEMIC, I accompanied the chief commercial officer of one of my clients, a multinational enterprise based in Europe, to their company sales event. The CCO, referred to as Jeremy for confidentiality purposes, had spent a year attempting to alter the company's messaging and positioning. His aim was to convey that the company was highly innovative and equipped to assist clients in adapting to rapid changes in their industry. Additionally, he wanted to emphasize the company's global presence and ability to bring cutting-edge innovations from all over the world to bear in local customer situations.

While at the sales event, we met with some of Jeremy's regional revenue leaders. To gauge the effectiveness of his messaging and positioning changes, he requested that each salesperson provide him with their elevator pitch about the company. Unfortunately, the results were disheartening. The salespeople spoke of the company's longevity since World War II, which suggested that the company was old-fashioned and set in its ways. They also mentioned the company's origins and deep connection to a specific region, as well as several random messaging points that Jeremy believed would only confuse and turn off their target customers. In essence, he heard the exact opposite of what he had hoped for.

About halfway through the meeting, Jeremy, although he maintained his professional demeanor, felt depressed. He couldn't understand why nobody understood their new corporate positioning and how to stay on message. What's worse, he knew there was a real cost. They were a legacy organization in their field and faced extreme market pressure from new, nimble start-ups. Sales and revenue were down, and they were losing market share. At the same time, they had multiple innovative solutions and had made big investments that were ready for prime time. Ultimately, they needed the new positioning and messaging to take hold and to accelerate revenue growth, especially for Jeremy to keep his job.

Jeremy's problem was that, while he generally knew what he wanted to communicate, he didn't have a story he could tell his team that showed how the company was innovating, and he didn't have a story he could tell target customers about how the company's innovation would help them. People understand and organize the world through stories. When you, as a leader, don't have a story, your employees will create their own to fill the vacuum. That's why he got so many people talking about the history of the company and its deep connection to a single region, with each of them telling their own stories with their own spins and points of emphasis, and all the varied stories didn't express just how innovative and progressive they were.

I call the issue Jeremy faced "random acts of conversation." And it wasn't just for his sales team. The marketing team for his company was producing "random acts of content" by building their own stories. Essentially, each team was doing whatever they wanted and trying different ideas, without a true overarching sense of what mattered to their customers. The team didn't have any idea how to communicate with customers in a way that inspired them to buy. Random acts of conversation and content can work—every so often, the stars align, and you might inspire your buyers to work with you. But not often enough. Usually, a customer will go through the sales cycle, not find anything that resonates with them, and leave uninspired. You don't get the business.

At a lunch break in the sales meeting, once the CCO had composed himself, we had a rich discussion about the importance of a Go to Market Narrative and how this would appeal to his customers, his marketing people, his salespeople, and his product team. He mentioned that solving this "lack of narrative" problem would be one of his top priorities, and he would "make budget" to solve this problem immediately. On the spot, he engaged me to help them get their story straight. Over the next few months, we worked together to develop a

Go to Market Narrative for their company, and the results were excellent. His revenue organization was trained in the new narrative and started using it in their selling conversations and content marketing initiatives. From a strategic standpoint, they went so far as to reorganize the entire organization around the solution we had framed in their new Go to Market Narrative.

Chances are, you might recognize yourself in Jeremy's story. As a business, marketing, or sales leader responsible for revenue growth, you likely face intense pressure. You might feel you are missing a key strategic piece of the puzzle as part of your go to market strategy. If you find yourself thinking, "I need a new message," or literally, "Our story sucks," then this book is for you.

My name is Bruce Scheer, and I have been honing a Go to Market Narrative model since 1995. I have used this model to develop and execute highly successful go to market initiatives with multiple industry leaders we all know, including Adobe, Microsoft, Dell, Citibank, HP, SAP, Unisys, McKesson, NetApp, Volkswagen, and others. I've also worked with numerous hyper-growth "scale-ups" to refine the model, including Concur, SuccessFactors, and Tableau, helping these hyper-growth organizations stand apart from the competitive pack and inspire their buyers to take action.

At its most basic, a Go to Market Narrative is deceptively simple. It's a story you tell a customer that shows the customer the problem they have, the outcome they should desire, and how, by working with you, they can achieve unprecedented success. This narrative then becomes the strategic backbone of the Go to Market Strategy. Everything, from product development and offerings to marketing positioning and sales conversations, can be designed to align with the Go to Market Narrative.

For all its simplicity, most organizations don't have a unifying Go to Market Narrative. Many companies don't even recognize that they lack a Go to Market Narrative. And those that do often make one of three major mistakes when trying to find a remedy.

In mistake number one, business and revenue leaders do nothing and continue with their random acts of conversations and content. To justify this approach, they say to themselves, "I hire good people to make meaning with our customers—why should I interfere?" This is the most common and worst trap to fall into. It costs companies millions of dollars and countless hours of labor every year. Often, it will cost you your job.

Mistake number two is delegating the task to "fix our message" to an internal marketer and expecting them to simply figure it out. The issue is that they often don't have the industry experience, customer world understanding, and acumen to craft an inspiring Go to Market Narrative. In short, they've drunk the internal Kool-Aid. Most are trained to create messaging for solutions and features, not overarching Go to Market Narratives. Even if they know how to think in narratives, they often lack the power to get the rest of the organization to buy in. Because the Go to Market Narrative becomes the strategic backbone of the company, it usually needs to come from the top, developed in conjunction with workers from all levels and across departments. If you assign this initiative to a mid-level manager, chances are they will waste time and energy on a narrative that only a small part of the company uses—if you are lucky. The goal is alignment and consistency in messaging. That requires leadership and collaboration across siloes.

Mistake number three is bringing in an expensive brand agency. Left to their own devices, an agency will go off and develop a clever catchphrase and an associated message map. But this still isn't a Go to Market Narrative. Emotion spurs humans to action, and the best way to achieve that is through a Go to Market Narrative.

This book provides a simple, step-by-step model to develop and deploy a compelling Go to Market Narrative. The stakes for this are huge. Nobody can afford a go to market misfire. If your organization has made a strategic investment in your offerings and your people, it's time to maximize the market opportunity with a compelling Go to Market Narrative.

CHAPTER 1:

EMBRACE THE NARRATIVE IMPERATIVE

SIMPLY PUT: the best narratives make the customer, not the vendor, the hero. These narratives show the customer that they have a problem and what life would look like if that problem went away. Then, the narrative shows the customer how they can use your solution to overcome their problem and achieve incredible success. You, as the vendor, should be the sidekick, not the hero. As they say: always a Robin, never a Batman.

In my experience, few companies comprehend the importance of a narrative as a catalyst for driving revenue growth. Often, those who do, don't know how to craft a proper narrative. When most companies tell stories, they cast themselves as the hero. They focus the story on how they built an awesome solution or how they became a "market leader." This is especially true in the tech field, where most companies are started and run by delightfully nerdy people who love to geek out about their products and associated specs. I refer to this as solution-centric orientation because it focuses obsessively on products, features, and specifications. You are the hero, and your story is focused on you and your "stuff."

It's possible that you're guilty of this as well. Take a moment to click through your website and review your home page. Do you primarily feature solution-centric product content, or do you focus on the customer and their challenges? How many pages are dedicated to talking exclusively about yourself? How often do you showcase your products and their features? If you have a narrative, where is it located? Is it tucked away in an "About" section that customers don't often visit?

There's a time and a place for solution focus. This content still matters—it showcases your competencies and capabilities, and it elaborates on how you can bring your buyer to the promised land. Still, for most companies, the solution-centric approach dominates the conversation and prevents a buyer-centric narrative from forming.

The importance of a buyer-centered narrative cannot be overstated. Early in my career, a client brought me in to help develop a Go to Market Narrative for his software solution. We did so and then ran focus groups with the target audience to test the narrative. Afterward, one participant came up to tell me that he had previously been through a sales cycle with my client and had decided not to buy. He told me, "What I heard before sounded nothing like this, and now, this seems way more important to the success of my business." That same day, he contacted my client to continue the conversation and quickly became a customer. It was the same company, same needs, same product. The only thing that changed was how we discussed the solution in the context of a Go to Market Narrative.

If I can get philosophical with you for a minute, I would like to talk about the big *why*—why I am passionate about my work and the impact I'm seeking to achieve by writing this book. The lack of compelling, clear narratives represents a colossal drain on society. Most B2B organizations only close an average of 40 percent of the deals that enter their pipelines. Think about all the wasted time in meetings, the wasted money on salaries and ad buys, the money left on the table when deals disappear, and all the would-be customers who lose the value they would gain by buying. I see such a huge opportunity to impact the way buyers buy and the way sellers and marketers sell through the addition of clear, compelling Go to Market Narratives. It makes everything so much easier when the dots are connected.

To bring us back to your situation, a clear and compelling Go to Market Narrative will help you to bring focus to your revenue team. Suddenly, they can clearly articulate the overall strategy from the customer perspective, including what buyers to target, the central problem you solve, the outcome you promise, how your solution guarantees that outcome, and how the buyer can continue to buy. You can do this in a clear, simple fashion. They don't fumble for words. Everyone—each marketer, salesperson, content creator, and associate—knows exactly what themes to hit upon in their work. This isn't to say that everything they do becomes scripted—they have the freedom to riff as long as they hit the central themes of the story. Overall, this alignment with a Go to Market Narrative leads to many benefits, including greater marketing impact, better selling conversations, faster sales cycles, better deal close rates, better solutions, more customer referrals, and ultimately, accelerated revenue growth.

In the abstract, a Go to Market Narrative seems deceptively simple. You will craft it around your ideal client profile and target buyers. You will spotlight their Big Problem that your Big Solution can help them solve. Then, you will promise them a Desired Outcome. Next, you will introduce the Big Solution in a simple way that they can quickly comprehend. You will then prescribe next steps.

That's it. Simple as it seems, few have mastered this. If you look at fifty websites, you might identify one that comes close to this model. A Go to Market Narrative will help you stand out, inspire your buyers, and accelerate revenue growth.

For the three main components—Big Problem, Desired Outcome, and Big Solution—I want you to try to think on the largest possible scale. In the B2B world, you're usually selling to executives, and you're usually selling something that costs them thousands, if not millions, over time. To get an executive's attention and to get them to part with that kind of money, you need to do something big. This is another major issue with solution-centric advertising. Nobody cares about the nifty little aspects of your solution. They care that it solves a problem, that it saves them time, that it makes them money.

For that reason, I find it useful to think about the above narrative attributes as themes, or essentially as umbrella ideas.

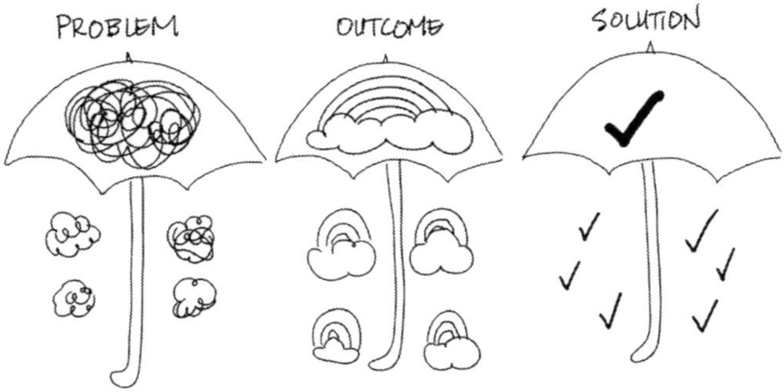

When you articulate your customers' Big Problem, try to articulate their most important problem in a way that contains all the smaller problems they have. In the coming chapters, we go into detail about how to craft each of these big themes, but for now, it can be useful to think about it through a medical lens. When someone has strep throat, they suffer from several symptoms, such as sore throat, fever, and fatigue. "Strep throat" is the Big Problem; it's what needs to be fixed and fixing it will resolve everything else. The Desired Outcome they're looking for isn't to get rid of each symptom—it's to be "healthy." And the way they do that isn't by a patchwork of mini solutions (such as ice cream for the throat, pain killers for the fever) but through the Big Solution of "treatment," which may include a doctor's diagnosis, antibiotics, painkillers, and bed rest. A solution-centric narrative often deals with a multitude of "mini" symptoms. An effective Go to Market Narrative diagnoses and treats the actual root "Big Problem." And executives like to solve "Big Problems" versus "Mini Symptoms."

Here's a personal story to further explain this concept. One day in the spring of 2020, in the early days of the COVID-19 pandemic, my oldest brother called and told me that our dad wanted to sell his boat and needed help listing it on Craigslist. I responded, "Crap, this means I'm selling his boat." We both knowingly laughed. My dad was in his nineties, and while amazingly cogent, he was completely illiterate regarding the internet. My old man still used snail mail, and since both he and the boat were four hundred miles away from me, any attempt to list and sell it online would require endless phone calls and close coordination.

After a short silence, my brother said, "Hey, I'm wondering if you might want to buy dad's boat."

I responded, "Are you kidding? Does it have a 49-inch ultra-wide hi-resolution monitor on it? Is it infused with advanced navigational tech, including night vision and radar and sonar? Can it drive itself like my Tesla? Is it emissions-free? If none of that, why in the heck would I want a nasty, polluting old fishing boat?"

Here he reminded me that he was still the older and wiser brother and possibly the better salesman, even though he'd never carried a sales bag in his life. He started with a simple question. "So, how long have you been living on that island?"

I responded, "Sixteen years. Why?"

He paused a while for effect, then simply said, "If I were living on an island for all that time, I would just feel trapped."

He paused again. I replied incredulously, "What does that even mean? Why would I feel trapped?"

"Well," he said, "If I were on an island without a boat, what if something bad happened? Let's say another outbreak. Let's say the ferry system somehow totally breaks down. Let's say, and God forbid, the earthquake that's expected in the Pacific Northwest sometime over the next fifty to five hundred years finally hits. What then? Where would you and your family be? I don't know about you, but I would feel trapped!"

I let this sink in for a few moments while thinking to myself, "Drat. He might have something here." But I waved off the concerns, told him I'd call dad, and got off the phone.

Luckily, this happened on the weekend, because I didn't sleep the entire night. I tossed and turned, ruminating about being trapped on the island. I had a family to protect. The next day, I called my brother back and mentioned, "Hey, I think I might be feeling trapped. Tell me more about that boat. How would I use it if I bought it? Would I be able to get out and about? Isn't it kind of small for being out on the waters of the Puget Sound?"

He responded, "Well, you would have to go slow in rough waters and stormy conditions, but for all intents and purposes, if you use it safely, it technically has enough draft to get out and about in the open waters. And on that island, there are tons of places to go with it. You are sitting in a boaters' mecca. There's probably at least one marina per mile in your area. You can explore different ports, and most of the ports have amenities and nice restaurants, cute shops, and tons of history. I'd imagine you would have a ton of fun exploring the surrounding areas. And your wife, I'm sure, would love trying the different foods each marina had to offer."

Now I was getting excited, but I knew the old adage. The happiest days in a boater's career are the day they buy the boat and the day they sell it. I asked for more details about the boat—its age, condition, and value. It seemed affordable. He also provided tons of guidance on how I could easily dock it and use it, and that was it. I was sold.

The next weekend I drove a few hundred miles to go pick up the boat. I had a fun negotiation with my dad, paying him more than he asked for, and brought the old fishing boat all the way back home. And my family and I, in the dead winter of the pandemic, went out on it at least five times a week, rain or shine, exploring the different ports of call in the Puget Sound area. About a year later, we flipped the old fishing boat and moved on to a Boston Whaler. And we are far from being done having fun exploring and boating.

My brother, operating on instinct, guided me through a perfect Go to Market Narrative and started it by making me the story's hero. He wisely identified the **right target buye**r—a buyer with the propensity to buy and the right conditions for his solution. Me. I had money, lived on an island with ready access to many boating launches, owned a vehicle with a trailer hitch, had a place to store a boat—but had no boat. In essence, I was "pre-qualified."

Then, he nailed my **Big Problem** in one word: trapped. After that, he helped me see the **Desired Outcome** in three words: **fun and adventure.** Instantly, I felt a deep desire to move from being trapped to living a fun life filled with adventure exploring the Puget Sound. And he gave me the **Big Solution** to the problem: boating. Then he dove into the details of the solution. He spent lots of time honestly explaining what I was getting into—how the old fishing boat was in great condition, how I would learn to use it, how it would fit in my current living situation, and how I would spend time and money on maintaining it. We then talked about the **next steps** and how I would go out and pay for it, bring it home, store it, and care for it.

And that was it. My family and I have been puttering around the Sound in a boat ever since.

Questions to Embrace the Narrative Imperative

- How have you approached the "imperative for narrative" in your go to market strategy to date?
- How would shaping a compelling, consistent Go to Market Narrative play into your overall go to market success?
- Who is on point for ensuring you have a compelling, consistent Go to Market Narrative as part of your go to market strategy?

CHAPTER 2:

TARGET THE RIGHT BUYERS

JUST BEFORE THE COVID-19 PANDEMIC, I spoke with a close friend who was struggling to sell an English as a second language learning technology platform in China. He thought there would be a huge demand but wasn't getting the uptake he and the board of directors expected. I asked him to explain in four or fewer words what he was selling. He described the product as an "English language platform." Then I asked him to describe in four or fewer words the outcome he promised. He said, "Confidence." I asked why, and he explained that the platform helps students learn English faster, giving them confidence in their fluency, which would help their careers.

"Well," I told him, "I definitely see a potential fundamental problem. You might not be focused on the right target audience. Do the students actually *buy* the platform?"

He immediately realized that they did not. The school administrators decided whether to buy the platform, and the students merely used it. Yet he and his company had created an entire narrative designed to show how the platform would help students. To tell a great story, the first thing you need to figure out is: Who is the hero? You can have the perfect narrative, but if it's not geared toward the people who can buy what you're selling, you'll never sell anything.

To figure out your exact target buyer, think about the leadership roles of the buyers who most often buy from you. Or, if your solution is new to the market, think about the people in the organization who will have the greatest desire and ability to buy your solution. Most often, they will be the people who sign the contract with you. Identify their area of responsibility in the organization. Is it a functional area? Is it a particular cross-organization initiative? What are these buyers' typical titles?

A lot of sales and marketing experts talk about the need to build consensus on a buying committee. Essentially, this theory states that anyone who might have a say in the buying decision needs to be targeted and convinced by the sales and marketing teams. However, in my experience, targeting everyone who might play a part in the decision can ultimately muddle your message. It is better to target a few key decision-makers and then let them build consensus with their colleagues. They know more about their colleagues and what matters to them than you ever will. To quote sales strategy expert Steve Martin, they are the "bullies with the juice." They can convince the buying committee to move with their decision, but only if they *truly* believe in what you're selling. In other words, if you inspire them with your narrative, they will fight for you to the end.

Questions to Target the Right Buyers

- Which buyer persona(s) will be the ultimate decision-makers? Who will sign the contract with your company?
- What are their areas of responsibility?
- What do they care about in terms of their goals, key challenges, and the metrics by which they measure success?

CHAPTER 3:

SPOTLIGHT THE BIG PROBLEM

WHEN SPEAKING WITH NEW CLIENTS, I often start with this question: "What are you selling at the end of the day? A problem, a solution, or an outcome?" I receive varied responses, but most often, people say, "Our solution." This makes sense. As we have covered, almost every company relies on this solution-centric selling model.

Really, it's a trick question. To sell anything in a B2B context, you need to sell all three. And the order in which you sell them matters—a lot! First, you must convince a buyer they have a problem, that there is an outcome that will be possible if they solve their problem, and finally, that your solution can help. Think about it: Who cares about a solution if they don't even know they have a problem? In short, a solution is an answer to a problem. And who cares about a solution or a product if they don't know what exact outcome that solution will help realize?

So, you have to start with the problem, and that problem needs to be big enough for an executive with serious buying power to care about. You need to articulate it in a way that allows your target buyer to instantly understand and identify with the associated challenges and struggles. Yet, when I ask business leaders to tell me the Big Problem they solve, I often hear a laundry list of "little" problems. When I push them to settle on one clear Big Problem, they usually say, "But we serve so many customers and solve so many problems that it's impossible to boil it all down to one single Big Problem."

I understand where they're coming from. It can be incredibly difficult to identify one Big Problem. But it's not impossible. I have helped multibillion-dollar enterprises boil everything they solve down to one Big Problem. Doing so allowed them to create much more powerful content marketing and hold more productive sales conversations.

So, what we are trying to do is boil all the little problems down into a single Big Problem and *name it* in four or fewer words. I refer to this as "spotlighting" the Big Problem—lighting it up as bright as possible while keeping everything else out of sight.

Let's look at an example. In 2018, I met a younger man named Toni (name changed to protect the innocent) at a hotel bar. Toni mentioned he had a newly minted MBA from the University of Southern California and was in San Francisco with his CEO, attending a healthcare trade show. I told him I was a corporate broken story fixer, or BS Fixer™ for short. He laughed and asked if he could test his story with me.

I said, "Of course," and asked what he sold.

He launched into a long explanation of his one-product company, which he eventually summarized as "virtual reality technology for doctors." I knew this would be fun—here, clearly, was a solution-centric corporate story in need of fixing with a Go to Market Narrative.

As always, I started with the target buyer and asked, "Are the *doctors* actually buying the VR?"

He laughed a little and said no. I asked him to describe his solution a bit more. He mentioned it places doctors in a virtual reality surgical environment where they can hone their skills. I asked which buyers he got the most traction with, and he said it was usually chief medical officers at hospital systems who made the decisions to buy. Engaging them was the fastest path to sales success.

I asked about the hospital industry's context. He explained that there are senior doctors, junior doctors, and interns who work together on each surgery. Often, there is more patient demand than the senior doctors can manage. To make matters worse, the senior doctors usually don't trust junior doctors and interns to play a role in the surgeries, much less to lead surgeries on their own. Therefore, the senior doctors do most of the surgeries on their own, stretching themselves even more thin.

Because the senior doctors face all this pressure, they often don't do their best work, which causes post-surgery complications and costly repeat visits. Often, hospitals face lawsuits as a result of poorly performed surgeries. Toni then explained that the VR technology would help train junior doctors and interns so that they could take pressure off the senior doctors, who would, in turn, perform better. We had identified several small problems—patient harm, lawsuits, repeat hospital visits, and tired doctors. But the Big Problem was that the whole clinical team wasn't performing at the level it should. We knew what the Big Problem was, but now we needed to name it in four or fewer words. The name we came up with was: "underperforming clinician teams." This was perfect—we could explain how it cost the hospital tons of money and how, left untreated, it would only get worse. And this term also contained all the smaller problems—including a negative brand reputation, subpar patient outcomes, and surgeon burnout/turnover. But we had one compelling, big idea that we could sear into the customers' brains and make them desperate for help.

In general, identifying the Big Problem requires a keen understanding of your buyers' world. You need to look at their market dynamics. What external trends are creating pressures that your solution can help them mitigate or take advantage of? Then, look at their internal imperatives. How can your solution help them reach their goals? What challenges do they face that your solution addresses?

Once you have figured out all that, determine how much it would cost the company not to move forward with your solution. For example, I did some narrative work for a large e-commerce managed services provider. They helped brick-and-mortar stores such as Dick's Sporting Goods set up online selling operations. In the narrative we created, we highlighted the fact that the cost of doing nothing for their prospective buyer was monumental. Within just a few years, they would cede almost all their online market share to Amazon. And with Amazon moving full steam ahead, literally, the laws of physics would not allow these brick-and-mortar entities to recover. As history shows, many of them went out of business, such as Toys "R" Us.

Think of challenges that are getting in the way of your target buyers that your solution can address. You will be thinking about the pains and costs of the external trends and pressures, as well as the internal business imperatives and challenges, if the buyer doesn't change. Fast forward the clock a year or two and see what that will cost the buyers and their businesses. You can then characterize the whole Big Problem state and name it in one, two, three, or no more than four words.

Questions to Spotlight the Big Problem

- What are your main external trends that create pressure for your target buyers?
- What are your buyer persona's goals? What are their frustrating challenges that your solution can resolve?
- What is a Big Problem central theme you can name in one, two, three, or no more than four words?

CHAPTER 4:

ENVISION THE DESIRED OUTCOME

AT THE CONSUMER ELECTRONICS SHOW in 2019 in Las Vegas, I saw John Chambers, former chair and CEO of Cisco Systems, give a talk about the importance of being able to see patterns within and across industries, connect the dots, and realize huge opportunities. John also talked about his perceived disability of being dyslexic and how he leveraged his condition as an advantage. While he might not be the world's fastest reader, he can rapidly see patterns, connect the dots, and capture market opportunities—giving him an "unfair advantage." Under his leadership, Cisco grew from $70 million in annual revenues to approximately $40 billion. After the talk, I was chatting with a very senior sales leader at Cisco, and John approached us for feedback. He was curious to know how his talk about messages landed. We said that the talk was excellent, and we continued talking. Eventually, the sales leader asked, "John, what's your number one piece of advice you would give to other sellers?" John, famous for leading executive-level selling conversations as a CEO, responded, "That's easy. Don't sell products; sell outcomes!"

I agree. Most sales and marketers want to move straight from the problem to the solution. But that skips an important step. Spotlighting the Big Problem ratchets up the customer's pain. And before you move on to the solution to the Big Problem to take away their pain, it's much better to help them envision a Desired Outcome and vicariously experience the pleasure they will feel once the problem goes away. By doing this, you're pulling on two essential buying levers at the same time: pain and pleasure. Effectively, the goal is to create tension between the Big Problem state and the Desired Outcome state. The more tension between these two states, the more discomfort the customer will feel and the more excited they will be to explore an answer that will make their Big Problem go away and allow them to experience the Desired Outcome state.

For example, let's return to the VR for doctors case. We discovered that the Big Problem was "underperforming clinician teams." To find the Desired Outcome, we asked: What will life look like without that Big Problem? As always, we needed to name the Desired Outcome in four or fewer words. We started with the antithesis of the problem, which was "high-performing clinician teams." The VR solution could guarantee high-performing clinical teams—it allowed junior doctors and interns to rapidly gain the skills they needed to perform surgeries without supervision.

But "high-performing clinician teams" wasn't a big enough Desired Outcome, especially for the key buyer in their go to market strategy, the chief medical officer. The key question to ask here is: *Why* does solving the Big Problem matter to the chief medical officer? How does solving the Big Problem help the chief medical officer and, ultimately, their organization? What does having the solution enable the chief medical officer to achieve? For the chief medical officer, the immediate thinking was that high-performing clinician teams serve patients better. We needed to come up with a name for this Desired Outcome state in four or fewer words. We landed on "better patient outcomes," as that was a phrase most chief medical officers sought to achieve. Like with any theme, this served as an umbrella that contained several smaller outcomes: happy patients, healthy patients, happy staff, greater staff retention, fewer insurance-claim tussles, fewer lawsuits and negative media exposure, and greater profitability. In other words, everyone would win.

A great way to validate if you've named the right Desired Outcome is to think about your target buyers' mandate. In the B2B world, people buy solutions to do better in their jobs. In this case, our target buyers were chief medical officers. We knew their mandate was to help their institution stand apart with a badge of honor by driving better patient outcomes, so we knew we had hit on the right Desired Outcome.

Questions to Envision the Desired Outcome

- Who are your target buyers, and what are their critical mandates?
- What are the top-level benefits your buyers will realize after your solution is in place?
- What is the Desired Outcome central theme you can name in one, two, three, or no more than four words?

CHAPTER 5:

SHOWCASE THE BIG SOLUTION

USUALLY, WHEN I GET A BUSINESS LEADER to talk about their solution, it feels almost impossible to get them to stop—especially if they had a hand in shaping the solution! It is the moment they have been waiting for. They love their solutions, and because most companies are solution-centric, they have spent hours thinking about their solutions. But even though they love to talk about the solution, few know how to do so effectively. Most business leaders talk about their solutions regarding features, functions, and benefits. They brag about the cloud and analytics capabilities they offer, their state-of-the-art cybersecurity practices, or their unmatched customer service.

This misses the mark. By now, the customer will know the Big Problem and the Desired Outcome. They will want the outcome so badly that it hurts. The Big Solution is the bridge that will bring the customer from the problem state into the outcome state. That means the Big Solution must operate at the same high, thematic level as the Big Problem and Desired Outcome. Any discussion about the product and service features and functions should come later. To illustrate what I mean, let's return to our example about VR for doctors. In this case, the buyer was the chief medical officer. Their Big Problem theme was "underperforming clinician teams," and their Desired Outcome theme was "better patient outcomes." Originally, the company had called their solution "virtual reality for doctors" because that's what they sold. But that is a product, and it operates at too low of a level to connect to the

Big Problem and Desired Outcome. Using "VR for doctors," the narrative would have read something like this: "By using our VR for doctors, underperforming clinician teams can create better patient outcomes." This narrative hardly makes sense, and it requires more explanation.

The best way to name the Big Solution is to answer the question: *How* does my product move the customer from the problem state to the outcome state? In this case, the answer was that the VR allowed doctors to receive more training more quickly without harming patients. As always, we needed to condense that into four or fewer words, and we ultimately settled on "experience without risk."

With this Big Solution, the Go to Market Narrative reads as, "When young and/or underperforming clinician teams rapidly gain experience without risk with our technology and services, they can immediately create better patient outcomes." This is coherent. Each part connects to the others, and it makes a compelling promise to chief medical officers.

As with the Big Problem and Desired Outcome, "experience without risk" is just a theme. It's a playing field that allows a salesperson or a marketer to discuss all the specifics of their solution. It will also allow the product team to think about other products and services that will help deliver on this promise of "experience without risk" for future product sprints.

After you've given the buyer the narrative, and when you're elaborating on it in a meeting or piece of content, you can go into detail about all your features and offerings. At this point, you also want to address all your differentiators.

One of my good friends and clients once lost a huge deal to Amazon after putting in months of effort selling the customer on their Go to Market Narrative, simply because they didn't do a good job differentiating their solution from the rest of the playing field.

I recommend that you find three attributes that showcase your solution strengths and, of course, name each attribute in four or fewer words. You can then explain what each attribute is and why it matters from the buyers' perspective, and you can offer some proof of how you delivered each attribute for other customers in similar situations.

For example, this part of the narrative in front of the chief medical officer might go, "Now to enable the solution, experience without risk, we help you put into place several key elements, including our virtual reality technology; our proven game-based, micro-learning curriculum; and our customer enablement team dedicated to making sure your solution is successfully implemented and you meet your objectives and achieve your Desired Outcome. We also set up a dedicated Slack channel for your doctors, and we offer X, Y, and Z. You get the picture. Now let me tell you the three key attributes of our solution that make it different from other approaches and alternatives in delivering better healthcare outcomes. The first is our doctor-centered learning approach. What this means is the learning experiences we design are tried and tested with a panel of highly experienced senior doctors. We make sure not only the learning efficacy is spot-on, but we also ensure they love the learning experience."

And so on through the other three differentiators so the prospect recognizes that you're the best person to deliver the results they need.

Questions to Showcase the Big Solution

- *How* does your product move customers from their Big Problem state to their Desired Outcome state?
- Can you describe your Big Solution in one, two, three, or four or fewer words?
- What are three key differentiators about your Big Solution?

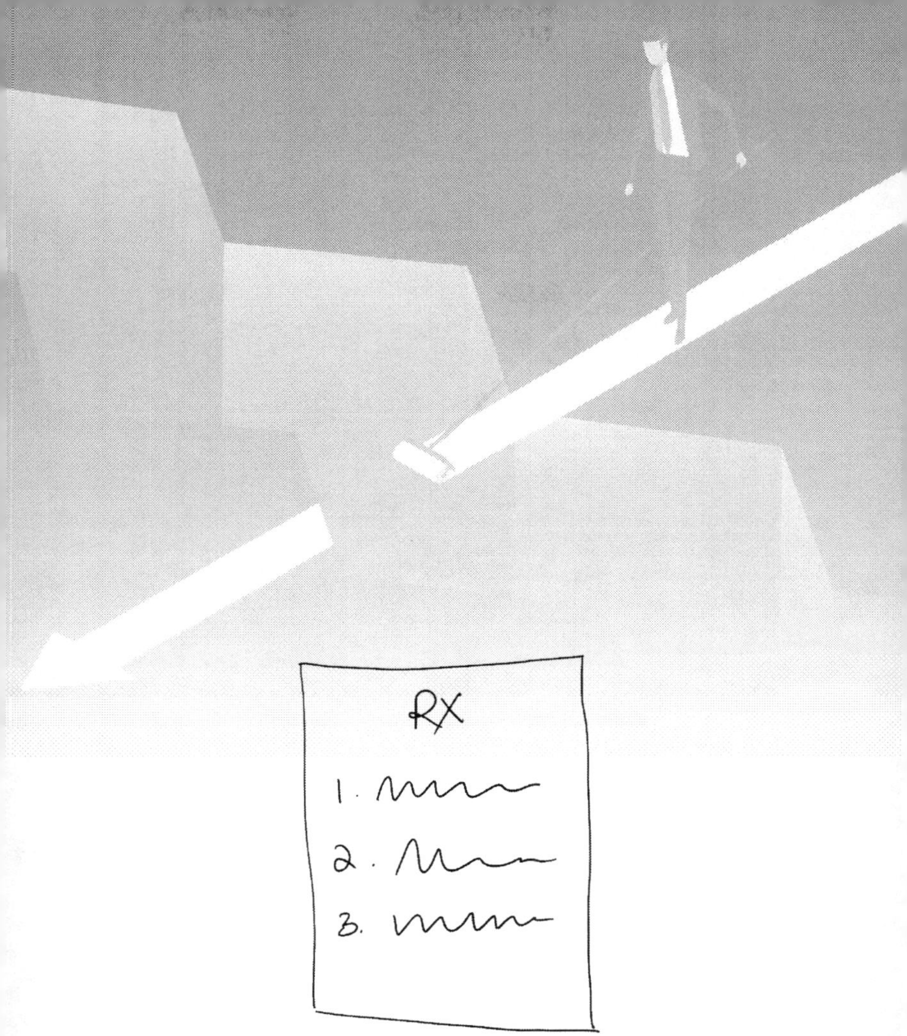

CHAPTER 6:

PRESCRIBE NEXT STEPS

SINCE 1995, I'VE WORKED with thousands of salespeople and marketers, and I've seen thousands of them make the same blunder. At the end of a meeting, I hear them ask some variation of, "So, where do you think we should go from here?" The buyer often responds with something like, "Send us more information," or, "We will have an internal meeting on this and get back to you," or, worst of all, "Send us a proposal, and we will consider it." I see the same issue in content marketing pieces, which usually end with a shallow call to action that doesn't inspire the customer to go on a journey with your company.

In American football, a "fumble at the goal line" is when the team on offense loses the ball right before they score and gives it to the other team. Suddenly, the offense is on defense, and they've wasted all the time and effort it took to get to the goal line—and that's exactly what these salespeople are doing. Up until that fateful question, the seller was in control. They had the ball, took it all the way to the goal line, and were about to score. But then, they gave control back to the buyer, and now they're playing defense. Suddenly, the seller must scramble to send more information; waste time crafting a proposal and chasing the buyer to see how the internal meeting(s) are going, if they are going at all; and ping them to see if it is an opportune time to talk again. This is a horrible place to be in—for both parties. Buyers don't like to feel chased, and salespeople expend way more energy than they need to. The same dynamic plays out in marketing. The content inspires the buyer to buy but doesn't prescribe concrete steps to close the deal.

Instead of the above approach, I teach my clients to arm their sellers and marketers with clear next steps. This is the only part of the sales practice that I recommend crafting and then "hard coding." In most cases, the closing process for a customer will be more or less the same. Having the steps in the buying process packaged instills confidence in buyers. They can see that you have guided many buyers before them through the process in a simple, painless way. Once you have this in place, a salesperson can end a call by saying, "Based on my experience, I would recommend that we take X, Y, and Z actions next. Does that work for you?" I also recommend spelling out some simple next steps on your website. Each next step should have a defined objective, set of activities, participation expectations, decisions to be made, and stated deliverables.

Your prescribed next steps will be unique to your solution, but the overall goal is to help your point of contact get their colleagues to enthusiastically support the deal. This often includes a meeting between the seller, point of contact, and anyone else involved in the decision-making process. After that meeting, quickly follow up with an assessment that showcases the expected emotional, operational, and business value associated with the change. It also includes more great reference stories, a business case, and some form of proof of solution concept. Sometimes it includes "art of the possible" mini-workshops or executive briefings that define the why, what, how, who, and when that shape the solution roadmap.

It's impossible to overstate how much of an impact packaged "next steps" can have. As part of the earlier iterations of the frontline partnership between HP and Microsoft, they hired my team and me to do some work with their joint sales and marketing teams. I asked each team what next steps they had in the can, and very few had any at all. I made them all develop clear next steps, and their close rates for the targeted solutions rose to over 50 percent for customers who started selling conversations. In 2005, the marketers from HP won the HP Marketing Program of the Year Award, in no small part because they knew their next steps could help them stay in control and keep everything moving forward in driving revenue growth.

Questions to Prescribe Next Steps

- What are the typical and potential next steps your buyer can take to accelerate their buying journey?
- What is the objective, set of activities, participation expectations, decisions to be made, and deliverables for each of these next steps?
- How can you frame up your next steps in up to three broad categories if there are more than three next steps?

CHAPTER 7:

VISUALIZE YOUR NARRATIVE

IT'S A CLICHÉ: a picture is worth a thousand words. And like many clichés, it contains a kernel of truth. This one happens to be backed up by science. I've seen the following statistics: the brain processes visuals sixty thousand times faster than text, and 90 percent of information transmitted to the brain is visual. Because over 50 percent of how we interpret the world is through visual cues, visual information plays an essential role in memory formation. Our visual bias shows up in our behavior, as tweets with images receive up to five times the engagement of those without.

All of this is to say that well-crafted visuals can communicate your Go to Market Narrative far more effectively than language alone. A meaningful image will leave an emotional impact on a prospective buyer that inspires them toward action, draws attention to the most important elements of your message, and helps the audience understand your point. As an added benefit, working on visuals will hone your thinking and your narrative even more.

While I recommend that you build images for most pieces of content, most people can tell their entire Go to Market Narrative with only two images: a Big Problem state visual and a Big Solution state visual. To prove how potent a well-crafted image can be, I'm going to show you, without any context, the visuals that one of my clients produced.

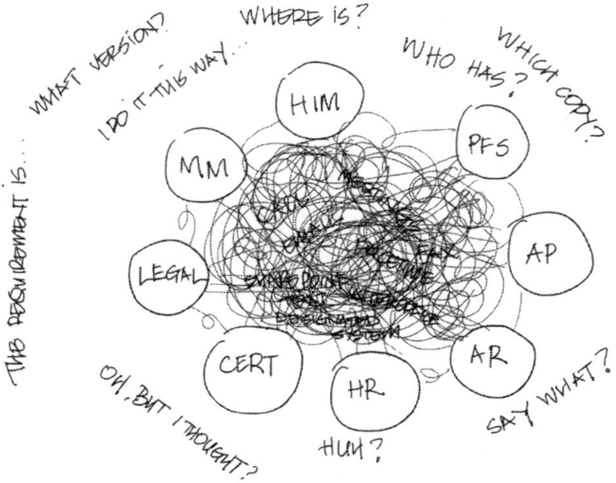

Big Problem

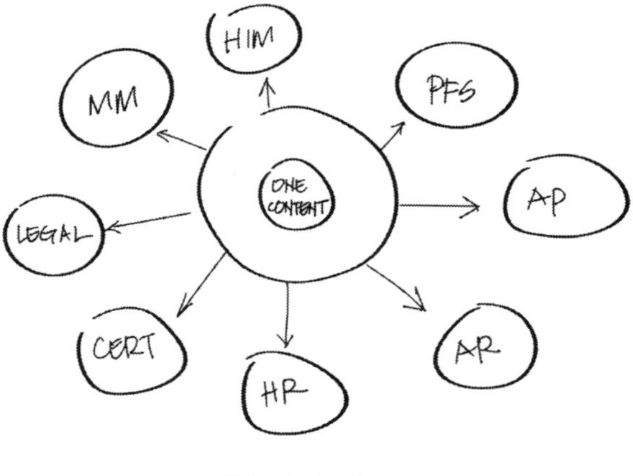

Big Solution

Without knowing anything about the company, you can get a crystal-clear narrative from these two images. The problem is one that anyone who works in just about any sort of organization knows all too well: chaotic, poor communication. My client's solution allows for clean, calm, and productive communication. Everyone knows what everyone else is up to, balls don't get dropped, and the organization can thrive. Also, pay attention to how each image makes you feel. The Big Problem image is stressful—you can hardly read the text; it draws your eyes in several directions. One of my former clients called the Big Problem image "the big ugly," and the example above is plenty ugly. In other words, it inspires pain. As the world-renowned consulting guru Alan Weiss says in his book *Million Dollar Consulting*, "Logic makes you think, and emotion makes you act." The pain the customer feels will inspire them to act, so the image should inspire as much pain as possible.

The Big Solution, on the other hand, looks beautiful. It's clean. It's aesthetically pleasing. Who wouldn't want to go from that messy Big Problem state to that beautifully organized Big Solution?

That example comes from my client McKesson, which was trying to sell an IT collaboration platform called OneContent to hospitals. To generate those images, we asked ourselves: How can we depict the buyers' Big Problem in a way that allows buyers to instantly recognize their situation while also providing new insights? We did a few mockups and then looked for ways to make it even uglier, adding the intersecting lines in the middle and a lot of the words on the side.

For the Desired Outcome and Big Solution images, we started with the question: How can we depict a simple and beautiful desired state using the visual vocabulary we have already established? That last part is key. Notice how, in each image, the basic building blocks are the same—circles to show each department, lines to show how they communicate. This creates continuity—it allows customers to see how they will transform by working with you. Ideally, this image communicates how the customer can attain their Desired Outcome thanks to the Big Solution.

Finally, notice how simple each image is. In my experience, the best visual narratives are simple enough to be sketched, and I even encourage my clients to sketch out the narrative for prospective clients during meetings. A sketch seems like a living document. A glossy visual, on the other hand, feels (and is!) completed. When you sketch the narrative in a sales meeting, it allows the buyer and seller to truly co-construct the narrative, and it helps the buyer truly make it their own. The buyer starts to own the Big Problem, Desired Outcome, and the Big Solution visualizations. In other words, by co-developing these images, they sell themselves your product.

As you start to craft a visual narrative, I recommend you aim for two goals: keep it simple and make it conceptual. Each visual should communicate the one big idea and nothing more. I often see people try to pack in extra details or find representations for specific quirks or features of their products. These distract from the main point and do more harm than good.

It doesn't have to be a full representation of reality. You want to illustrate the problem, outcome, and solution at a high level for your narrative instead of producing a complete schematic. The job of your visual narrative isn't to finely describe the buyers' situation but to get their understanding of and agreement on the problem you are solving, the outcome you are helping them realize, and the solution that's going to make the problem go away and help them achieve their Desired Outcome. The more detailed and exacting nature of a visual can distract and detract from your narrative purpose.

The best way to land on a visual narrative is an old-school brainstorm with flip charts and markers. Gather the people with the best understanding of your product, messaging, and customer needs, then give them all a marker. To start a session, I might search phrases for the concepts I'm trying to portray online and show the group the results as a starting point for inspiration. And then we doodle away until we find something great.

Questions to Visualize Your Narrative

- How can you visually depict the Big Problem your buyers face? How can you make the Big Problem state look even uglier?

- How can you visually depict the Desired Outcome and Big Solution? How can you make the Desired Outcome and Big Solution state even more beautiful?

- Is the visual contrast between the Big Problem state and Big Solution state creating enough tension? Will your buyers readily see themselves in the Big Problem state and desire with urgency to move to the Big Solution state?

CHAPTER 8:

TAILOR YOUR NARRATIVE

I OFTEN HEAR FROM MY ENTERPRISE CLIENTS something along the lines of "We are a large company with several organizations, subsidiaries, and divisions. We offer hundreds of products, target scores of buyer personas across dozens of verticals, and serve clients that work in a wide range of industries. Can one single Go to Market Narrative *really* appeal to all our audiences?"

The answer, if they've landed on the right overarching themes for their narrative, is always a resounding yes. But they must learn how to tailor their Go to Market Narrative to new circumstances. The good news is that a well-designed Go to Market Narrative will easily shift to cater to new situations and circumstances, saving you tremendous time and energy in creating fundamentally new narratives. A great way to test whether you have landed on the right Go to Market Narrative is to see if you can easily adapt it to appeal to all your target buyers. If you find that you need to dramatically change the narrative to, for example, convince a manufacturing company to buy your solution, then you haven't found your true Go to Market Narrative.

In many ways, the flexibility of the Go to Market Narrative is the entire point. Your "big rock" central themes will keep you on message as you traverse different verticals, organization types, and buyer personas. I recommend using your base Go to Market Narrative, tweaked by industry, if necessary, in conversations with the highest levels of your target companies.

If you go in to pitch to the entire board or the entire C-suite, then you likely will be talking to people with diverse backgrounds and business concerns. And most importantly, you'll be talking to executives who don't have time to get lost in the specific solution and underlying product details. They will care more about the Big Problem and Desired Outcome and how this might impact the bottom line today and tomorrow. The standard Go to Market Narrative will speak directly to this.

But before you ever reach the boardroom, you likely will have selling conversations with middle managers and VPs. These people will have much more specific concerns, and they will need to know not only the impact but exactly how you can bring about the impact. They also, as many people do, think their problems are unique. To best communicate with these people and to increase your odds of one day pitching to the C-suite or the boardroom, I recommend deploying a tailored Go to Market Narrative coupled with industry and buyer persona-specific substories.

To illustrate what I mean, let's look at an example. In 2005, the communications equipment company Alcatel-Lucent (ALU) hired a new leader for their $2.6 billion enterprise arm. The leader at that time, Tom Burns, surveyed the vessel he had inherited and saw many improvement opportunities. If this were a boat, it once would have been a beautiful mega-yacht, now cluttered with unnecessary appendages, eaten away by the sea, and covered in mussels. His sales team had *460* different products to sell. It was too many for any one rep to memorize and sell effectively. The marketing team was similarly overwhelmed—they couldn't tell what products or features to emphasize in their messaging. And that confusion ultimately extended to the buyers. Salespeople would engage in haphazard random acts of conversation, often pedaling whatever specific product they personally knew or liked the best.

But there was, under all that mess, still a beautiful ship. He just needed to rediscover it. Tom quickly realized that he needed a clear, unifying message, and he and his leaders brought in my team and me. We worked together with his heads of strategy, marketing, communications, and sales, plus multiple stakeholders, to shape their new Go to Market Narrative. We, as always, started with their target audience: large organizations with senior leaders who were frustrated that their company couldn't respond to key trends and pressures, that they weren't utilizing all their organizational knowledge, and that their internal processes were cumbersome.

We summed up all those complaints into the Big Problem theme of "moving too slow." The Desired Outcome ALU could promise these large, lumbering organizations was to become more dynamic, so they coined the Desired Outcome name "dynamic enterprise." The Big Solution that bridged the gap between the Big Problem and the Desired Outcome was the "dynamic communication framework."

Now, ALU served hundreds of clients across several verticals. The first step to tailoring their narrative was to adapt it slightly for each vertical. For example, they drew a lot of business from the public sector. To appeal to that audience, we shifted the Desired Outcome from "dynamic enterprise" to "dynamic government." Many people would find the phrase "dynamic government" oxymoronic, and in a lot of ways, it is. But that was part of the power of that narrative tweak. Government employees are well aware of their lethargic reputation. If anything, most government employees who must fight with the meat grinder of public bureaucracy every day will be the first to admit that their offices move more slowly than they would like. If we used a phrase like "dynamic organizations," it wouldn't have had the same pop. The government employees seldom hear themselves described as "dynamic," and the idea of a dynamic government was music to their ears and very aspirational.

ALU also targeted hospitality companies, and we used a similar change to the narrative for them, replacing "dynamic enterprise" with "dynamic hospitality." The next step was to develop industry-specific substories. In the hospitality example, ALU used as their starting point the Big Problem "moving too slow." They built the substories around changing customer expectations in hospitality, including the desire for mobile experiences and personalization. They also told substories about the need to drive internal improvements to raise the consumer experience while boosting business performance. They then told stories about other hospitality companies and how they had taken steps to shift to "dynamic hospitality" and the benefits they saw.

Now came the most challenging part. They needed to create substories about their Big Solution, "dynamic communication framework." Essentially, ALU needed to find a simple way to talk about the myriad products and services they offered. They wanted to do whatever they could to reduce sales complexity and highlight the bottom-line impact for each buyer. To do that, we made sure the substories didn't even mention specific products. As soon as you start talking about products, you're getting lost in the weeds. Instead, we focused on product categories. We asked ALU: What areas of a client's business do you most often improve? They responded that their technology helps employees work better, streamline processes, share knowledge, and operate in alignment with other teams in the network. We simplified this into four solution categories: people, processes, knowledge, and network. Then, when salespeople had conversations with prospective buyers, they could ask what specific problems those people faced in their day-to-day lives. The salesperson could then put that problem into one of the four categories and talk about how their solution helped the prospect see improvement in the area they were most concerned about. Later in the buyer's journey, the salesperson and buyer could work together to find the exact products and services to buy.

Note how the tailored Go to Market Narrative never strayed far from the core Go to Market Narrative structure. ALU ended up using this narrative for almost a decade, transcending several acquisitions and organizational transformations. During that decade, they saw accelerated revenue growth, and internal surveys showed that the campaign did exactly what we had hoped it would. After adopting the new narrative in the hospitality sector, ALU saw an 81 percent increase in brand perception. Fifty-nine percent of respondents were more likely to consider ALU for their business needs, 97 percent of respondents felt they clearly understood ALU solutions, and 86 percent felt they clearly understood the value of ALU solutions. Our work won praise from observers within and outside of ALU. We even won Corporate Executive Board's B2B Marketing Campaign of the Year award, specifically for how we tailored the narrative to speak to the hospitality sector. All of this was possible because we crafted a narrative that was simultaneously universal and unique.

Questions to Tailor Your Narrative

- What industries do you serve where having a tailored version of your Go to Market Narrative will improve your go to market effectiveness?
- What key buying audiences might be better served with a tailored version of your Go to Market Narrative?
- What substories will need to be developed for different tailored versions of your Go to Market Narrative?

CHAPTER 9:

ALIGN FOR SUCCESS

BACK IN 2008, I had the pleasure of working with a senior marketing leader and internal champion of a multi-billion-dollar business, Unisys. As the VP of Marketing at the time, he was instrumental in aligning key stakeholders with a new go-to-market narrative. We had developed a newly minted "big idea" Big Solution theme called "People Computing," which had tested well inside and outside the organization. Our internal champion was excited to present it to the CEO for his review and blessing. Unfortunately, the CEO didn't like the concept at first glance, making his disapproval known in uncomfortable terms. Our champion was crushed, and he called me to share the bad news and figure out our next steps.

I empathized with him and suggested that we take a different approach. I asked if he had shared the results of our target client validation with the CEO, and he said no. I also asked if he had discussed with the CEO how excited his sellers were about the "People Computing" theme, and again he said no. I even inquired if he had mentioned how analysts and third-party advisors thought the idea sounded fresh and differentiated, and once again, he responded negatively. This got me excited, and I proposed a plan of action.

We decided to make another attempt to persuade the CEO to appreciate the "Big Solution" theme. We emphasized that the go-to-market narrative development had gone through a rigorous process and was not designed with him in mind, as he was not the target buyer. Instead, we shared with him how much the target buyers we tested the "Big Solution" with had appreciated the narrative and how the concept was a "pure gold" message strategy. Ultimately, the CEO agreed to go with it and even fell in love with the "People Computing" concept. He promoted it within the leadership team, encouraging investment in the new go-to-market narrative. This successful outcome was just from one division, as the CEO later elevated the message strategy and go-to-market narrative to position the entire organization.

The key takeaway from this story is that prioritizing the opinions and needs of your target buyers when developing your go-to-market narrative can help you create a narrative that resonates with them, leading to positive outcomes, accelerated revenue growth, and avoiding potential missteps that can waste time, money, and energy. When you inspire and engage your buyers, you set the foundation for a successful go-to-market strategy.

So, back to you and your situation. If you are responsible for creating a go-to-market narrative but are not the leader of your organization, it's important to follow a disciplined and rigorous process to ensure that your narrative hits the mark and gains buy-in from critical stakeholders. An approach that I have found to be very effective is using the North Star Messaging Model, which is designed to help shape a compelling go-to-market narrative while gaining necessary stakeholder buy-in and excitement.

The North Star Messaging Model is based on the scientific method, which involves formulating a hypothesis and testing it to determine if it is valid and resonates with target buyers and other key stakeholders. This approach has been refined and tested since 2000, and it has been successful every time. In contrast, not following a disciplined approach can lead to go-to-market misfires, which can have negative consequences.

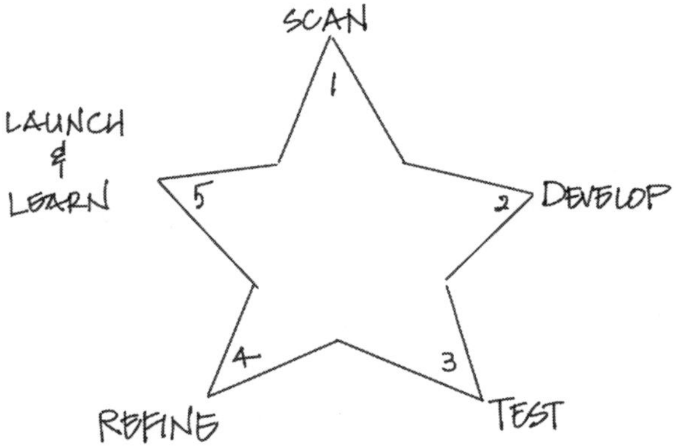

The North Star Messaging Model has five key phases: Scan, Develop, Test, Refine, and Launch and Learn. By following this approach, you can ensure that your go-to-market narrative is well-designed and effectively resonates with your target buyers and stakeholders, leading to go to market alignment and success. Let's review the key phases of the model.

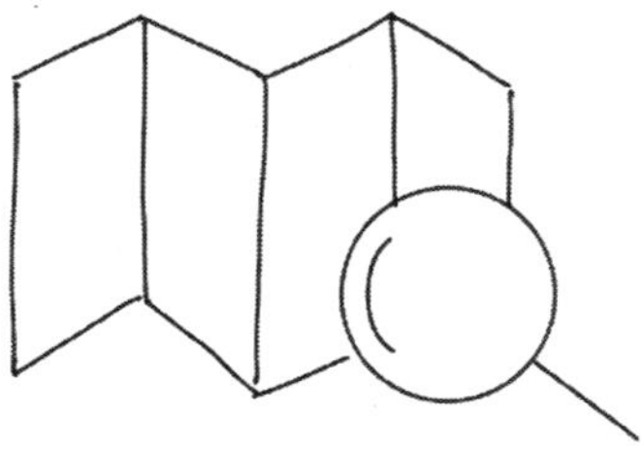

Scan

The objective of the Scan phase is to identify internal and external perspectives to ensure that your Go to Market Narrative is compelling, unique, and sets you apart from the competition.

During this phase, you gather input from key formal and informal leaders across your organization who possess a "customer world perspective." Seek out individuals who have worked for or with your target customers, and who understand the role of your target buyer. It's also essential to speak with those who have sold similar solutions into the target customer and to the target buyer. Additionally, the product or solution leader can provide valuable insights into the customer world, while staff who are servicing your accounts can bring unique customer-world insights to the table.

In addition to gathering internal perspectives, it's crucial to collect external insights from target customers, industry analysts, and influencers. This can be accomplished through a variety of web-based and primary research techniques. You'll also need to analyze your competitors' messaging to formulate hypotheses on how your Go to Market Narrative can stand out and resonate even more with your target customers and buyers.

Develop

The objective of the Develop phase is to create and align the key elements, sub-stories, and main visual narrative of your go-to-market strategy. To achieve this, a core team of customer world experts from inside and potentially outside of your organization should be brought together. During this phase, you review the findings from the Scan phase to help the team understand the problem domain of the target customer and buyer, both verbally and visually.

Next, you build your Go to Market Narrative, which includes conceptual visuals that spotlight the buyers' significant problem, envision the buyer's desired outcome, and showcase the big solution as well as high-level solution elements and prescribed next steps. To ensure that your go-to-market narrative is well-designed and effective, it's recommended to download a free go-to-market narrative assessment from inspireyourbuyers.com/narrativeassessment. This can be used as a quick safety check as part of your Develop phase before moving into the Test phase.

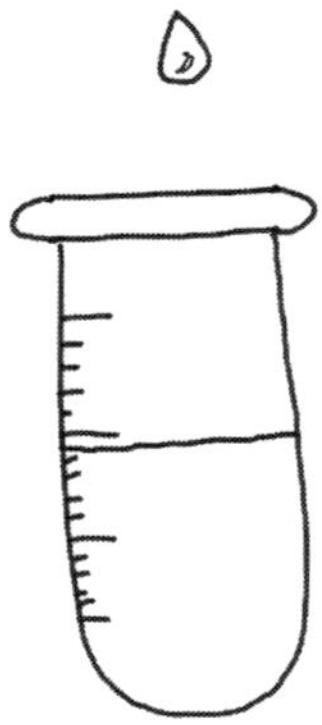

Test

The objective of the Test phase is to gather feedback from key internal and external stakeholders to ensure that your Go to Market Narrative is effective. This involves seeking input from sales leaders (both formal and informal), marketing leaders, product leaders, target buyers, and third-party advisors and analysts.

During this phase, you are looking to gather qualitative feedback that will help shape and refine your Go to Market Narrative. It's important to remain open-minded and receptive to different perspectives and opinions. Some feedback may be actionable and useful, while others may not be as relevant. By seeking feedback from a range of stakeholders, you can gain a better understanding of how your Go to Market Narrative is resonating with your target audience and identify opportunities for improvement. During the Test phase, it's important to capture quotes and statements from the feedback you receive. These quotes can be used to help gain buy-in from key stakeholders when you launch your Go to Market Narrative to a broader audience. By incorporating feedback from internal and external stakeholders and showcasing how their input helped shape and refine the Go to Market Narrative, you can build a sense of excitement and buy-in around the strategy. This can help ensure that the launch of the Go to Market Narrative is successful and well-received by the broader audience.

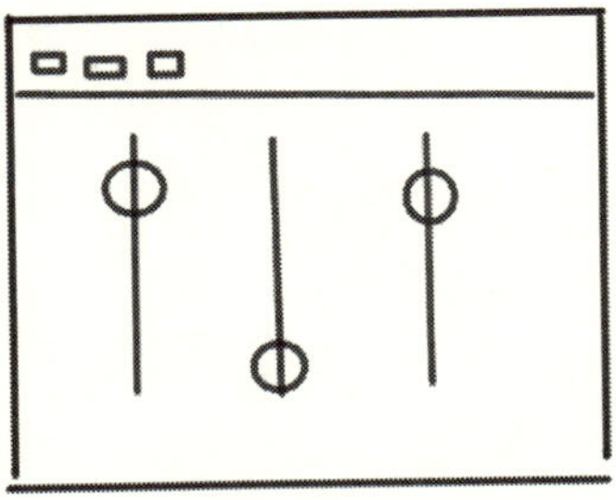

Refine

The goal of the Refine phase is to review the feedback gathered in the Test phase with key stakeholders, sift through the refinement ideas generated, and gain final alignment. This can be a tricky phase, as everyone involved may have different opinions. However, it's important to remember that the opinion that matters the most is that of the buyers. After all, the whole point of the Go to Market Narrative is to inspire change in the buyer. This is your anchor point.

When reviewing the Go to Market Narrative during the Refine phase, it's helpful to view it from the buyer's perspective.

This will ensure that the final product is compelling and resonates with the intended audience. Once you have conducted your final reviews and locked in your Go to Market Narrative strategy and visuals, it's time to fine-tune your assets for higher impact. This provides a powerful brief for your marketers and sales enablers to build on-target content, training, and selling tools. By prioritizing the needs and opinions of the buyers, you can create a Go to Market Narrative that is well-designed, effective, and resonates with your target audience.

Launch & Learn

The Launch & Learn phase is all about translating your new Go to Market Narrative into marketing content and selling conversations that inspire your buyers. This involves working closely with your sellers, marketers, and partners over time to ensure that your Go to Market Narrative is being effectively communicated and received by your target audience. It's important to put systems and disciplines in place to reinforce on-narrative content and selling conversations, and to gain real market feedback to sharpen your Go to Market Narrative and assets over time.

By following this rigorous process, you can avoid a go to market misstep and increase the likelihood that your central narrative will hit the mark and inspire your buyers to make a change. The process also helps to increase everyone's confidence and enthusiasm, setting you up for go to market success.

Questions to Align for Success

- Who should you be talking to and what information sources should you be referencing both within and outside your organization to gain perspective for shaping your Go to Market Narrative?

- Which stakeholder(s) should you involve early and often to ensure they don't derail your Go to Market Narrative initiative?

- Who are representative of your target buyers that you should reach out to early for scheduling narrative testing sessions? If your target buyers are senior in the organization, you need to start scheduling early to make sure to get on their schedules.

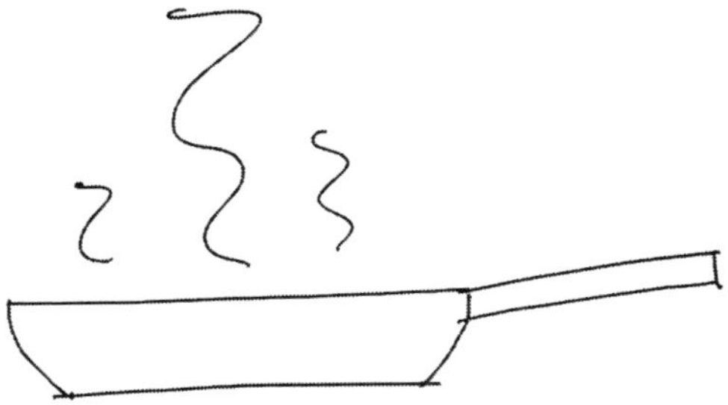

CHAPTER 10:

ENSURE YOUR STORY SIZZLES

WHILE DISCUSSING AN EARLIER VERSION of my book manuscript with a good friend, I mentioned my desire to assess the effectiveness of the go to market narrative. Neither of us had seen such an assessment before, but the concept of a "story that sizzles" resonated with me. It turned out that the word "sizzles" made for an excellent acronym and framework to evaluate the efficiency and effectiveness of a go to market narrative. At its core, a "sizzling" go to market narrative moves the buyer's mind and encourages them to change with you and your solution. To ensure your go to market story "sizzles," I am introducing the "SIZZLES" framework, along with a set of questions to assess your go to market narrative:

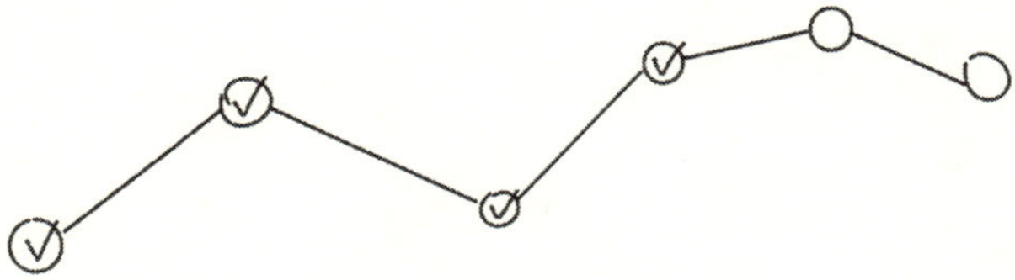

S stands for Structure.

Structure: the arrangement of and relations between the parts or elements of something complex.

Think about the structure of your go to market narrative. Is it developed around your target buyers' known or unknown big problem, and does it help them see their desired outcome and showcase the big solution? It should then prescribe next steps.

In short, it should follow the go to market narrative model you have read about in the preceding chapters. A former sales leader at Gong, a revenue intelligence company, mentioned a study finding they discovered after analyzing thousands of selling conversations. They found sellers are roughly thirty percent more effective and efficient if they have a story structure they are following. When you think about it, this finding makes excellent sense. A story structure can help improve selling conversations by providing a framework for organizing and understanding the information being presented and discussed. This can help the seller make more compelling arguments and anticipate the buyer's potential objections or concerns. Additionally, a story structure can help the seller stay focused and on track, making the conversation more efficient and effective. And probably the most critical point I can make about your go to market story structure is that it should follow the cognitive flow of the problem, outcome, solution, and next steps.

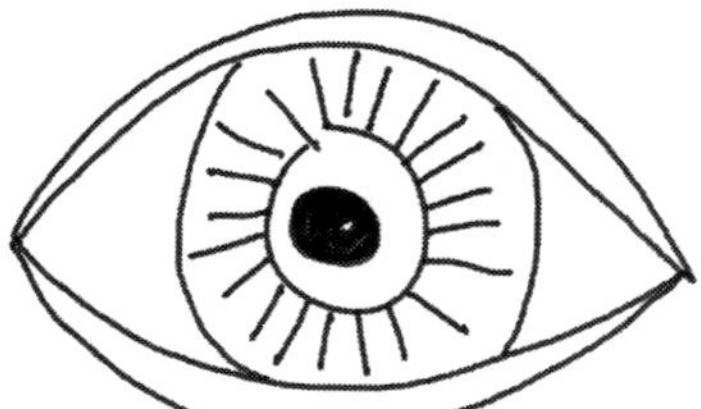

I stands for Insightful.

Insightful: having or showing an accurate and deep understanding; perceptive.

Does your go to market narrative possess insight? Does it introduce new and surprising ideas that teach your audience something about themselves or a situation that they were unaware of or did not fully understand? You will know that your narrative has been truly insightful when it exposes your buyer's blind spot or flaws in thinking in a manner that your buyer values. You can frame the problem in a way that the buyer has not seen before, or in a way that magnifies their problem's pain beyond their initial perception. The key takeaway is that your buyer should feel informed and educated after engaging with your go to market narrative.

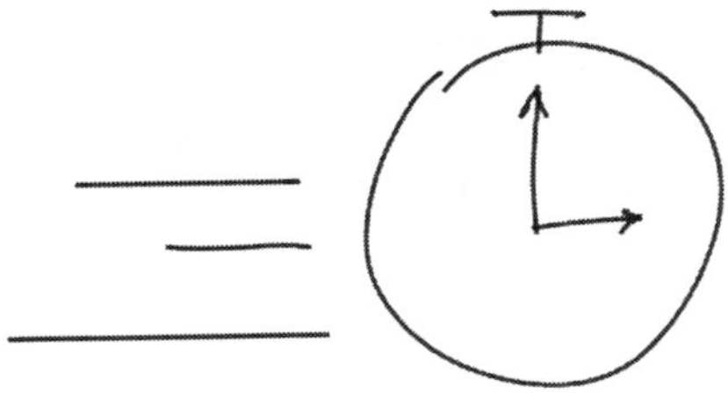

Z stands for Zippy.

Zippy: speedy, or bright and spirited.

When assessing your story, ask yourself if it maintains a steady pace and avoids being weighed down by excessive details. Does it "float without the bloat"? Does it efficiently use the allotted time for your audience, ensuring it doesn't end prematurely due to time constraints? You must ensure you discuss and agree on the final movement of your narrative flow: Next Steps! Your story should flow with the optimal balance of information and emotion to captivate your target buyer. When I think of "zippy," I visualize a compact sports car hugging the curves, moving swiftly from point A to point B, as efficiently and effectively as possible.

Z stands for Zappy.

Zappy: lively and energetic.

Does your story genuinely excite the buyer? Is it unique and innovative? Does your story instill buyers with the energy, enthusiasm, and conviction required to change their situation and proceed with you and your solution? If you have delivered an insightful narrative, as described earlier, you're already halfway there. The next step is to use the right words, energetic and motivational language, to help the buyer envision themselves in your go to market story, enabling them to transition from insight to action, from theory to practice.

L stands for Leading.

Leading: providing direction or guidance.

Does your story guide the buyer by helping them anticipate future challenges and, as the saying goes, "skate to where the puck will be," as famously quoted by hockey legend Wayne Gretzky? Does your story provide guidance on how to purchase and achieve maximum value when making the desired change? Does it highlight potential obstacles and offer solutions to address them? In the introduction of my book, I shared how my brother sold me an old fishing boat. He went beyond just promoting its features and benefits; he helped me purchase the "total solution," including towing it home, storage, care, and additional ways to derive value from it. As a friend once pointed out, the actual selling begins after the buyer says yes, at which point, you need to help the buyer with the purchasing process. Therefore, a critical element is anticipating buyer questions and facilitating the buying process. This is typically embodied in the story's final "next steps" movement.

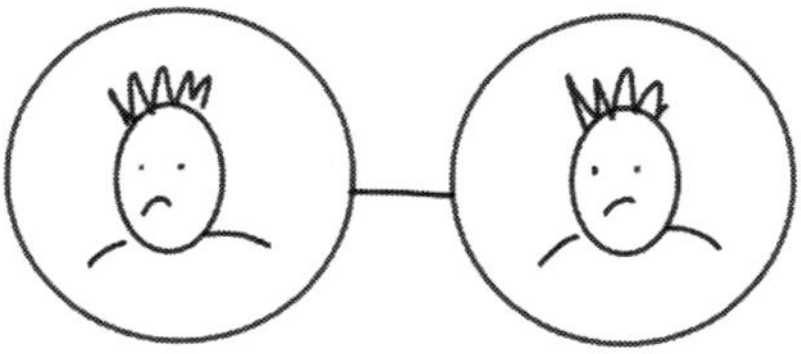

E stands for Empathetic.

Empathetic: showing an ability to understand and share the feelings of another.

Does your story feature enough "customer in similar situation" stories that depict the same problem state, emotions, and how they overcame it by using your solution, along with the results they achieved? It is essential for your story to empathize with the buyer's emotions and pain, which they feel after realizing the magnitude and consequences of their problem state. Your story should then resonate with the buyer's excitement and supreme satisfaction once they have achieved their desired outcome. By doing so, your story can instill confidence in the showcased solution and assurance in the buyer's abilities to overcome the problem state and attain the desired result using your solution.

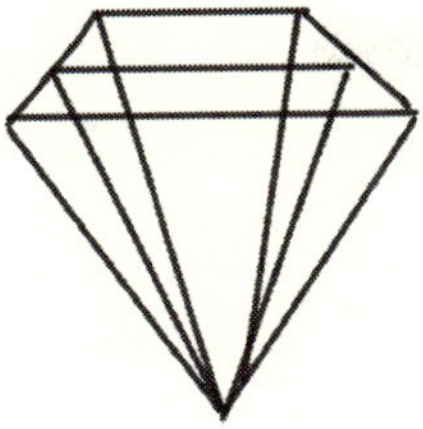

S stands for Sass

Sass: spirited, saucy, provocative, elegant, and sophisticated.

Is your story delivered with a touch of "sass," providing a peer-to-peer approach that builds confidence and trust with buyers, making them see you as a partner and backbone throughout the change journey? Do you convey through your story that you are more than just a vendor, but a strong partner? When I think of what "sass" means, I recall my late aunt Merle Crawford, whose extreme mental sharpness and inventiveness would shine through in her clever and apt humor. Merle never compromised her unique personality, but her wit, with a pinch of spice, was a joy to be around. She was always on your team, never subservient. So, does your story exude that kind of "sass"?

Now that you have the "sizzles" framework, you can run your go to market story through the "structure," "insightful," "zippy," "zappy," "leading," "empathetic," and "sass" filters to see what stays, what goes, and what needs to be added to help ensure your go to market story sizzles.

CONCLUSION

MY CLOSE FRIEND OFTEN SAYS, "Good on you, mate!" I echo the sentiment for reading this book. You have gained a unique perspective that few in the business-to-business revenue enablement realm have achieved, let alone applied. This same friend also poses the provocative question, "What's more important? Strategy or implementation?" This question typically elicits mixed responses. However, both aspects are equally vital. This book has provided you with the strategy. You have a model, practical examples of what "good" entails, and a development approach that works. It's time to either develop or redevelop your Go-to-Market Narrative or congratulate yourself for instinctively following this approach. If you plan to embark on an initiative, here are a few recommended next steps.

Educate Your Team

- ***Books:*** You will want to share the wisdom you've gained with others in seeking their collaboration and enthusiasm for crafting your new Go to Market Narrative. You can easily get them "on the bus" by ordering additional copies of this book and sharing it with them. You can do this by going to inspireyourbuyersbooks.com.

- ***Executive Briefing:*** You can book me to brief your team on the narrative imperative and how to develop a Go to Market

Narrative with an Executive Briefing session. For more information, visit inspireyourbuyersexecutivebriefing.com.

- ***Keynote Session:*** If you represent a larger organization with multiple solution development initiatives underway, you might consider bringing me in to conduct a keynote session at one of your upcoming revenue team events. For more details on what this looks like, visit inspireyourbuyersspeaking.com.

Engage in Go to Market Narrative Consulting

If the stakes and urgency are so high that you want me or my team to support you directly, please reach out to us at gotomarketnarrativeconsulting.com. We can discuss your situation and do a rapid assessment to make sure there is a good fit for us to work together to meet your needs and goals.

I hope you find these next steps useful. If the timing or fit isn't right for now, let's connect in the meantime at bruceatlinkedin.com. I wish you huge success in inspiring your buyers with your Go to Market Narrative.

ABOUT THE AUTHOR

BRUCE SCHEER is the President of InspireYourBuyers.com. He has applied and honed his Go to Market Narrative development model with industry giants such as IBM, SAP, Microsoft, HP, Oracle, Google, DXC Technology, Adobe, Infosys, Citibank, Alcatel-Lucent, McKesson, Motorola, and SITA, plus with "scale-ups" such as Concur, FinancialForce, SuccessFactors, Tableau, and others across the Americas, Asia, Europe, and the Middle East. He is a featured keynote speaker for industry and client events. He has worked with his clients to grow revenue and win industry recognition, including winning HP's Marketing Circle of Excellence and the Corporate Executive Board's Marketing Campaign of the Year awards.

Bruce's "personal why" is to inspire others to inspire others, and he yearly inspires thousands of revenue leaders, staff, and the buyers they serve with clear and compelling go to market narratives. Bruce has been a featured keynote speaker for large corporate events, including Microsoft's CIO Summit, and a guest speaker and educator for industry associations, leadership roundtables, in-company events, and ongoing programs across all major continents. He is on two boards of directors and is the incoming President of the National Speakers Association Northwest.

Bruce is an avid learner and a big believer in continuing education. He has attended the University of Copenhagen, Cornell University, the University of Hawaii, and the University of Oregon, where he was on the dean's list and earned his MBA. He has hosted and attended numerous executive development programs across the Asia-Pacific region with the University of California, Berkeley. He is based on Vashon Island in the Pacific Northwest in the summers, and you can find him and his wife in beautiful natural places across the globe during the winters.

To see Bruce in action, here's a link to a fun video featuring Bruce talking about the Big Problem, Desired Outcome, and Big Solution and in what order to sell each: inspireyourbuyers.com/funandexcitingvideo. Yes, Bruce had fun at the beginning of the pandemic, putting this video together. See what being stuck at home will do to you!

Made in the USA
Middletown, DE
10 December 2023

44211473R00061